LEARNING

TO

dance

ON

HOT COALS

*Juanita
Pero*

LEARNING
TO
dance
ON
HOT COALS

Juanita Pero

TATE PUBLISHING
AND ENTERPRISES, LLC

Published by Tate Publishing & Enterprises, LLC
127 E. Trade Center Terrace | Mustang, Oklahoma 73064 USA
1.888.361.9473 | www.tatepublishing.com

Tate Publishing is committed to excellence in the publishing industry. The company reflects the philosophy established by the founders, based on Psalm 68:11,
"The Lord gave the word and great was the company of those who published it."

Book design copyright © 2012 by Tate Publishing, LLC. All rights reserved.
Cover design by Lucia Kroeger Renz
Interior design by Glenn Rico Orat

Published in the United States of America

ISBN: 978-1-62024-742-6
Poetry / Canadian
Poetry / General
12.09.12

Dedication

This book is dedicated to my children, Shannon, Leanne, David Scott, and Apryl, who have enriched my life by allowing me to be part of their journey. Also to my faithful husband David for all his support and love.

Special thanks to my friends and co-workers at the Guelph General Hospital for their support and encouragement. I want to thank Mike and Mabel Gordon who got me started on this book and my good friends Bob and Linda Linton who helped in getting this book together.

Table of Contents

People

Faith/Religious

Miscellaneous

Introduction

This book was written as a result of a journey; a journey that could be called life but is more accurately called relationship. Getting to know myself has been part of the journey. As I get to know myself, I can relate to others. But most importantly, the journey has taken me to the feet of God, where I look up and am amazed at all I see.

As I come to know Him more, I am more at peace with myself, my fellow man, and life in general. Never will life fit into neat little slots, but getting to know God has helped me disregard the neat little slots and accept life as it is each day.

Faith that does not change a person, even to some extent the personality, is a dead faith. True faith reaches into the heart, changing thinking patterns, our very point of reference, and truly all things become new.

Most Holy God,
In reverence I bow before You,
In thanks I embrace You,
In faith I follow You.

People

LEARNING TO DANCE ON HOT COALS

Move quickly,
Step lightly,
Turn, dip,
Smile, focus,
Pray.

Head up,
Swiftly to the right,
Don't look down,
High step to the left,
Smile, focus,
Pray.

Life is difficult. Enjoy the good times. I handle hard times with motion. Accomplish something. Fill the house with good smells. Fill the house with music. That's my dance.

THE THINKER

She sits alone
And doesn't move.
She's not the type
That would intrude.

She listens 'til
It's all been said
And then she simply nods her head.

She calculates what's said and done
Adds the implications some,
And then she sees,
Within your soul.
Things you'd like to say aren't so.

She listens deep
To things not said
And paints the picture
In her head.

Some people seem to have an uncanny ability to see and understand—an ability that is a gift, a talent. If you have met one, you will recognize them.

FORGIVENESS

What did she mean by that remark?
Oh! That one thinks she's so smart,
She puts me down with every word,
I know, I saw, I see, I heard.

But in her heart where you can't see,
The things you heard weren't as they seemed.
If only we could believe the best,
Our hearts and minds would find more rest.

We assume we always know,
What was meant by so and so,
But if the words were as they seemed,
Forgiveness has always redeemed.

Many relationships have been broken needlessly by some careless remark or thoughtless action. God shows us the way to mend and restore by His example to us.

LONELINESS

Remember me?
We once were one.
Now I see you at a distance,
Laughing, hair wind-blown.

I don't know this new you,
I long for the person I knew.
There is a wall between us,
I feel it, you feel it,
Hands did not build it
Nor can hands remove it.

At times you face me
But your steps are backward,
Your eyes focus beyond me.
I cry, but you can't hear me,
I run, but I can't catch you.

So I stand alone,
Watching you go farther away
And I'm helpless to stop you.
My tears make you a blur
And I am alone.

To be lonely does not just mean to be by yourself. Being with someone who has separated their spirit from you causes a loneliness that is defeating.

The Relationship

Come to me,
Come to what I am.
I see you,
But the image you project confuses me.

I want to see you
Without defenses,
Without pretenses,
Without anything that isn't you.

Come to me,
Come to what I am.
Come just as you are.
So I may be what I am.

Expect nothing of me
And I will give you much.
Build no fabrication of me
For I can't live up to it.

Accept me as me,
With my faults and shortcomings,

With my hang-ups and flaws,
And you will be to me
What no one has been before.

Acceptance is something we all crave. Sometimes we try to be something we're not, just to be accepted. We even fool ourselves. No relationship can thrive under these conditions. We have to risk and trust enough to expose what and who we are. Then we have to be willing to love unconditionally when we see the flaws in others.

Off My Pedestal

I've come down off my pedestal.
I used to stand up high;
Be a good example,
Don't let them see you cry.

I've come down off my pedestal
And found to my surprise,
I never had them fooled at all,
They saw through my disguise.

I've come down off my pedestal
And they know I make mistakes.
I don't even try to hide it,
They'd know for sure it's fake.

I've come down off my pedestal
And, boy it can be fun
Grubbin' in your grubbies
When the work's not even done.

I've come down off my pedestal
And I let them see me fall.
If I don't, how will they know
It's God that keeps me tall.

I've come down off my pedestal
And they know I sometimes bend.
I've come down off my pedestal
And found a house of friends.

Setting a good example for our children is vital, but being a real person that our kids can relate to can get lost in our good intentions. They have to know that we get discouraged, angry, and fail. What we do with these things will be an example for their lives.

21

MOODS

The battle of the moods began
When my heart with God engaged.
Until that time I didn't know
A battle could be waged
Against these moods that came
Upon my life and captured me,
But that I was quite moody
Was so plain for me to see.
A bad mood just explained itself.
No one asked you why,
Just let you be and hoped a hope
Your mood would soon pass by.
Then God showed me a better way,
He said, "*Moods are a handicap,*
They're not part of my abundant life
They're just a selfish trap,
They won't bring you happiness
Life will pass you by"
Then He told me how and when.
Then he told me why.
Why it was the mood came on,
"*You think of only you.*"
When it was the mood came on,
"*You let yourself be blue.*"
The greatest thing He told me
Was the reason how.

22

How to these moods of gloominess
I didn't have to bow.
It narrows down to a great insight
And you surly cannot lose,
Everyday when you get up
You simply have to choose.

Feelings can rule our lives or we can make a decision to rule our feelings. My feelings will follow my thoughts so I say, "I can do all things through Christ who strengthens me." Phil.4:13. I believe it, I have proven it to be so.

MATURITY

Maturity has no finish line,
No point of completion.
There is no age of total maturity.

For to stop maturing
Would be to stop growing,
To stop learning,
To become unteachable.

Maturing is painful,
But in the pain there is a hidden joy—
The joy of knowing that at the end of the pain
We will have learned something.
Something valuable, yet priceless;
Something we could not have learned any other way.

Maybe the highest degree of maturity
We can attain in this life
Is to come to value pain and suffering.
Not that pain in itself is an end,
But a means by which we grow.

Age has no factor in maturing as a person. Some people can go through painful things and not be any wiser because of it. But we can use pain to look inside ourselves and see how we can be better people.

To Know Me

Hear me,
But not the words I speak,
For my lips will not betray
What is in my heart.

Touch me,
But not with your body.
Let me feel your understanding
Surround me and keep me warm.

See me,
But look beyond my face,
For the person I am
Is hiding in my soul.

There is a cry in all of our hearts to be understood, to be appreciated for just who we are. I believe it is extremely precious when we have such relationships. But more than this is each day, with each person we meet, to accept that particular person as someone valuable, to have the attitude and ability to look beyond the outer shell.

CHASING RAINBOWS

I built a foundation for my house,
Built it strong and square,
Put all my energy in its walls
So I could nestle there.

It was firm,
Would hold me up
If ever I should fall.
But my finished house I could see
I didn't want at all.

I want it round and made of dreams
But it's too late to change.
Tear down the loving,
Strong-built walls
And make a round, light frame.

A light round frame
Filled up with dreams,
But it would never hold,
For all its beauty and its charm
The storms of life would tear it down,
Its walls would quickly fold.

For what I want and what I need
Are not the same at all.
I need these strong, firm walls around
To catch me when I fall.

Choices have to be made. Our lives are not islands. We connect with many other lives. Our choices could destroy others even when it gets us what we want. Temptation is like a world of dreams. It promises so much. But James 1:15 says, "When sin is fully grown it produces death." In the temptation stage, it is not fully grown. May we always choose the strong, firm foundation of God's ways.

A GOOD MAN

What a good man I have married.
I know this because I watch him.
Completely different from me in every way,
He communicates in ways I fail to understand.
I misread him,
Coming to conclusions that aren't true.
But sometimes he gives me clues
To who he is;
Not purposely, but accidentally,
In a look, a gesture, a prayer uttered.
I have to be attentive
Because he hides himself well
Which makes him look selfish,
Most of the time it's not selfishness.
But survival he seeks,
So I give him space and time.
I forgive him for things
He's not guilty of.
I continue to observe;
Sometimes I understand.

This was written for our fortieth wedding anniversary. I have come to realize that the man I married is not the man I think I know. My judgments of him are often harsh and really off the mark. He is very non-verbal, so I'm left guessing and reading between the lines.

FRIENDS (AN ATTITUDE OF HEART)

You're my friend, so I release you, let you go,
You're my friend so I release you to let you grow.
For if I held you close, the way I long to do,
The love I have for you would not be true.
For a selfish love holds close, and smothers life,
But an honest love lets go and won't entice
You to take another way for me;
Hoping, all the time, that you won't really see
That my love for you is something that I need.
You're my friend, so I release you to let you grow;
But before I do, there's something you should know,
I accept you as God made you,
With the special gifts He gave you,
Even though I don't always understand
Why you think the way you think, I won't judge you.
Why you do the things you do, I won't condemn you.
You're my friend, so I will love you,
You're my friend so I release you,
No strings attached, my friend, I let you go.

This poem is called "Friends," but I think it applies to all relationships—our children, our spouse, anybody close to us. Unconditional love allows people to receive the best from us, and to give the best of themselves back to us in return.

30

Things That Can't Be Changed

Oh, the grief
And oh, the pain
Of things that can't be changed.

"What if only,"
"I wish I had,"
But things just can't be changed.

Sleepless nights
And tears of sorrow,
For things that can't be changed.

We wrestle with the angel,
We struggle in our soul,
And find we've been made stronger,
By things that can't be changed.

This poem was written for a very young person who was maimed in a very serious accident. Years later, I found the truth of the poem had become a reality. This person used his disability to become a strong athlete and travel the world.

Choosing

I've always thought that our relationship
Would never change.
There seemed no need for change.
But now I realize we both grow,
And change is a necessary part of growth.
If we try to hold on to what we have,
Putting our relationship in a vacuum
Or on a pedestal,
Ignoring any problem,
What we have would become artificial.
We have to look at each problem,
Then each other,
Leaving the other free
To again make that choice
To walk away or work with what we have.
Every time we choose "us,"
Over ourself,
We build something a little stronger;
Something more lasting and beautiful
Than before.

Building a beautiful relationship takes a long time, but it is well worth the pain it may cause us at times.

LETTING GO

As you've grown
I see how very individual you are;
A completely separate person from me.
When you were little,
You were a part of me,
But now, you belong to you.
My love for you will never change,
But my pride in you has grown;
My respect for your choices has increased.
You hear the beat of a different drum.
A different path you tread.
With love I say,
Walk on, my child.

It takes time to see ourselves separate from our children. It is usually a painful process for all. Relationship is the result.

A MASTERPIECE (ROY'S POEM)

Valuable things take time to create.
Slowly, patiently, the artist
Works to produce a masterpiece.
Lovingly adding minute dabs of colour
That would not be missed,
But when added,
The whole picture comes alive
Taking on a different meaning.
So it is with you.

Your creator is slowly,
Lovingly adding to your life.
At first it may look quite drab,
Nothing much of value,
But as He continues,
Beautiful things appear.
Surprising value is discovered,
Strength and character develop
That will serve you well.

Yield to His hand.
Patiently endure the mundane,
Enjoy the ordinary,
Be steadfast in the difficult.

For the Creator
Is shaping a masterpiece
Unique and priceless.

If we could see our lives this way, we would have more patience with ourselves. This was written about a young man in his teens who, because of his faith, grew into a strong and faithful husband and father.

An Innocent

An observer of life,
More than a participant,
Carried along by time,
But a true survivor
In every sense of the word.
She understood with her heart
The power of a hug,
The importance of gratitude,
And how to capture your heart.
Things many wiser people miss,
Things many wiser people fail to understand,
Things intrinsic to her nature.
One of the innocents of this world,
One of the cherished of the next.

This poem was written for a disabled person whom I came to know and respect. Disabled in many ways, she was still able to communicate love, touching many hearts.

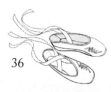

TAKE OFF YOUR MASK

I'll take off my mask
And you will see
Me, being simply me.

You take off your mask
And I'll see too,
You, being simply you.

Loving you with that mask
Has always been quite a task;
But when your heart is open for all to see,
To my surprise, you're just like me.

What joy we deny ourselves and others when we offer the world
our mask instead of who we really are.

37

A SAFE PLACE

A safe place,
That is what you are to me.
A place I can let down
All the walls
I have erected
To protect myself.

A place I can reveal
All of who I am,
And know
I will not be ridiculed
Or rejected.

A place of encouragement,
Where I draw strength
To face whatever tomorrow brings.
A place of comfort and peace,
Where I can grow strong,
So I may in turn
Be a safe place for you.

When we fall in love we become a safe place for each other.
However, staying a safe place is harder. It takes not only love but
also commitment and maturity.

A FRIEND'S DEATH

Quietly
I watch you,
Seeing past what
Has been done to you
By things beyond your control.
Seeing the essence
Of who you are to me.
Seeing that part of you
That has shaped
Who I am.
Seeing that part of you
Which has touched others.
Knowing that part of you
Will live on forever.

How hard it is to lose someone dear to us. To watch disease take and distort the person we know and love. Then to continually see and hold fast to the real person they were and will always be to us.

GRANDCHILD

I see you there,
The very essence of innocence.
I wonder how anyone
Could be more beautiful.

You turn to see me;
A look of pure delight
Fills your face.

You run to meet me,
Never have I been
More loved.

Never has anyone
Made me feel this important.
Surely some cosmic cycle
Is being completed
When I hold you,
My grandchild.

Nothing can prepare you for the feeling of parenthood. Likewise, nothing can prepare you for your first grandchild. The experience repeats itself with each new little person that comes. Not enough emphasis is put on the importance of the extended family. With broken families and relationships, we all lose.

TO YOU

I'm grateful that you are in my life.
My life is richer because of you.
Without people we can relate to,
Life would be an empty shell.
A shell that echoes hollowness.
A song that is monotone,
No high notes or low.
A dance of one step,
No dips or twirls.
But because your heart is open to me
Sharing good times and bad,
Victories and defeats,
We have together created
A melody and dance
We both know and love.
You have made my life
So much fuller.
I would have been so narrow
In my thinking,
If your thoughts were never shared,
So limited in my methods
If I hadn't seen you at work.
I have learned from you.
By being just who you are
You have allowed me to be
Just who I am.

Because of you I have been
Changed forever.

People we interact with have input into ours lives, especially people who are different than us. To value that input and the person that gives it makes life rewarding and rich.

WASTING TIME

Don't waste your time
Believing lies
That have been spoken to you,
By life,
By society,
By your own insecurities.
Believe that you are unique,
Believe that you are strong,
Believe that you can reach your dream.

Years go by and we stay stuck in old patterns because we have never challenged old ideas about who we believe we are. God says we are precious in His sight. Do we believe Him?

Seeking Spirituality

I had a cast
A form so smooth,
It was set
Had many rules.

I called it spirituality,
It was the ultimate goal for me.
I thought I knew
Just how it looked,
Refined and clean
Lived by the book.

But every day it let me down
This spirituality that I'd found.
Angry, I threw my mold away.
Stamped it down, gave up the day.
Then and only then I found
True spirituality could not be bound
By rules and molds or set in stone.
It had no face to call its own.

I found it in a little child,
In the weary face of an old man's smile,
In a dirty hut, a prison cell,
A mother's face I knew so well.
True spirituality does exist,
But oh, it is so easily missed.

Does spirituality have a face, or does it have many faces? How often we miss what is truly God because our idea of what we think is good can be so influenced by culture or background. The spirit of God can lead us to truth in all things.

Gaining Ground

Since we first met,
Much time has passed,
Friends at first
Then much more.
A deep understanding
Has grown between us,
Something solid and very tangible.

Battles have been fought,
New ground has been conquered.
Walls that looked unyielding
Have been torn down and forgotten.
Love and commitment
Has been stronger then the foe.

Now we have reached a calm place,
The turbulence has passed for now,
There is a unity between us,
A warmth, a friendship
That is full of contentment and love,
A time of refreshing.

There may be more challenges ahead
But past victories will give us confidence,
Bridges built, will hold.
Together we have made each other stronger,
Together we have become more complete.

Long term relationships take work. Our marriage has been through many struggles. With faith and love, we celebrate what we have accomplished.

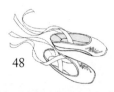

HEROES OF A DIFFERENT SORT

We look at some men and we say,
"What a hero! He saved the day."
Strong and mighty willing to give their lives
So others have a chance to live.
But there are some people that are just as strong,
Each day choosing right against wrong.
Against tremendous odds they wage their war,
Battles they have not faced before,
Poverty, sickness, a handicap,
Resources within themselves, they must tap.
Their minds, their bodies, each day they contort,
To become heroes of a different sort.

For many years I have worked with people who have faced defeating challenges each day—people I came to respect and admire. Their will to live life to the fullest of their capabilities was inspiring.

A Glimpse of Soul

A man of great stature
Lies in a bed.
Strong and defiant,
Angry at a foe he cannot see.
But a foe who has changed his life.
Sickness and pain is his enemy.
Changing who he was
Into what he now is,
Defensive and bitter.

A gentle hand
Is laid on his shoulder.
"I can help you my friend,
I stand with you in your pain.
I believe your battle is real."
Bewilderment—then acceptance
Flash in his eyes.

As a mantle falls
From a new work of art,
So the defensiveness and anger
Fall from this man.
Tears of humility come,
Exposing a gentle heart,

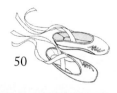

Who has suffered much,
And I see,
The beauty of this man's soul.

How easy it is to judge by first impressions. We all hurt at times and need compassion and understanding. How wonderful when we find it. What an amazing difference it can make.

51

THE VIEW

As children we are formed
By life around us.
A foundation is laid
Lasting for the rest of our lives.
We build on this foundation
With the things we experience.
How we view life,
How see others,
Is taken from this view.
It's the only view we have,
Other people see different views
But we cannot grasp that view.
We don't understand them.
We have to look from our view
And try to interpret life.
Loving, caring parents
Give us the best view.
Even though flawed themselves
Their love and kindness
Form a foundation under our feet
That we can stand firm.
Viewing the world
As a safe place.

I wrote this because I see so many people who still carry the scars of childhood into adulthood. It's not their fault—Would I have been any different under the same circumstances?

You're Stronger Than You Think

You're stronger than you think,
See what you've done 'til now.
You've earned your daily living,
By the sweat upon your brow.

You're stronger than you know,
Don't let doubt have its say.
Move forward in this moment
Your foe must move away.

It's no small feat to rise each day
And face the mountains tall.
Knowing if you stop for breath,
Your life begins to fall.

So march on to the drum
Whose beat you hear,
'Though to others may seen wrong,
Let faith and hope in you abide,
The God of love is at your side,
The world needs your victory song.

Nobody but ourselves knows how difficult we find life. Each day of our lives we fight to be victorious over our own demons. We need to give ourselves more credit. We can be our own worst critics.

A Mother's Prayer

Help me, Lord,
To respond to the changing
Needs of my children.
Help me to know
When to comfort,
When to scold,
When to hold tight and protect,
And hardest of all,
When to let go.

You are the perfect Father.
I want to be more like You,
But my fear gets in the way.
My selfishness hinders me.
Sometimes, I just want to walk away.
I'm tired, and I've had enough.
But each time my love for them
Draws me back;

Much the same as Your love
Led You to the cross.
True sacrificial love means pain,
But as I bring my pain to You,
I become strong.

Strong enough to lead my children
In the way they should go.

The hardest job in the world has been given to the most inexperienced. We learn, and we grow. We make mistakes, and we suffer. Our love is the only sure thing.

MORE

I believe there are people
Who deserve more than they have.
People who are better than most,
But have been dealt a hand in life
That has somehow changed the course
Of what could have been.

Good, faithful, hardworking, kind people,
Who because of one choice, one event,
Live a life that is in many ways
Less than what they could have had;
Less than they could have achieved.

Nothing can change this path they are on.
And even if something could now change it
The path would still forever be different
Than the original path
Their lives would have taken,
Because of the choice, because of the event.

Many succumb in small ways, some completely;
Shipwrecks of the life they could have had.
Others sail on smiling,

58

Sometimes forced, often genuine,
Always at great cost.

These are the people who hurting people
Connect with, identify with, feel safe with.
These are the people whose depth of wisdom
Takes you by surprise.
Not in a showy, "I'm so smart" wisdom,
But wisdom that gives you hope,
Wisdom that imparts strength,
Wisdom that washes away guilt,
Wisdom that lets you know
This lesser path they walk
Is in many ways more.

Difficulty and defeat can create a very positive work, changing us for the better.

Plastic Christians

I tried to please the people,
I just couldn't let them see
The imperfections in my life
Were just too much for me.
I tried to be like great men of God,
I thought that would do the trick.
Be strong and faithful, humble, pure,
I was sure that some would stick.
Now sticking virtue to your life
Is quite a messy job.
Charades will leave you empty,
Pretense, a certain snob.
You'll look shiny, new, and plastic,
Quite a stirring effect;
People-pleaser that you've become
They may never really suspect.
But God can't work with plastic men,
Organic is His style.
It may take a little longer,
But it's really worth the while.

When we try to be what we're not, it becomes hard work. We suffer, others suffer, and it hinders a true work of God in our lives.

SPEAK TO ME OF LOVE

Speak to me of love
Early in the morning
Let the sparkle in your voice
Brighten up my day.
Speak to me of love
Early in the morning
Let the sun break through
Before I'm on my way

Speak to me of love in the morning
Gentle and so soft against the
Roar of day.
Speak to me of love in the morning
Let me take those words throughout
My busy day.

Speak to me of love
Early in the morning.
Let me hear your voice
Gentle and so sweet.
Speak to me of love,
Make the burden lighter.
Let your gentle strength
Start me on my way.

Speak to me of love
When the storms of life are raging,
Let the nearness of your voice
Bring a comfort and a calm.
Knowing that with you
I have found a safe place,
Knowing where you are
Is where I now belong.

After a frustrating time of trying to get the children out the door and to school on time, I spoke some harsh words. After the children left and calm returned, I regretted it. These words dropped in my heart. It is my children speaking to me, and me speaking to God. This is a song, the second stanza is the chorus.

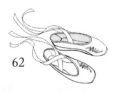

MY CHILD

My child, you delight my soul.
The sound of your voice
Falls pleasingly upon my ear.
Your smile fills me with joy,
My burdens become lighter.

My child, you cause my outlook
On life to change.
You are a solid force in a land
Of destruction.
Your tiny hands give me strength.

My child, may I cause you no pain
As I guide you in the way to go.
So when you have grown,
You will choose the way
Which gives you the things,
My heart craves for you to have.

Children are God's promise of a future. They are our motivators.
Nothing changes us more, causes us to work harder, brings more joy,
brings more pain, than our own child. Children are blessings from
God, often in disguise.

Faith/Religious

BALANCE

In a village not very far away,
Balance was its name,
Two neighbours lived side-by-side
But were not at all the same.
One neighbour's name was Liberty,
He felt he was so free,
He didn't have to listen to what affected you and me.

His neighbour's name was Law,
He lived a life of many rules
And if you were to challenge him
He could be as stubborn as two mules.

Now I'm sure I needn't explain to you,
They didn't see eye-to-eye
And to live together in Balance
Was, at times, trying they wouldn't deny.
The village of Balance was owned by Flexible,
That really wasn't his name

But they didn't know what to call him
For he was never always the same.

One time he seemed to agree with Law
The next minute Liberty,
For Flexible was flexible as anyone could see.
He said he was led by the Spirit,
Whatever on earth that meant,
He just seemed to have the right answer,
No matter what the event.

You see, Liberty was always
In trouble with Law.
He couldn't do anything right.
Law was always unhappy,
His life, a continuous fight.
Liberty thought he had such freedom,
He was always on Law's land.
What he didn't see was his freedom stopped
Wherever Law's land began.

And so the feud goes on and on
There never seems an end
To the problems they seek answers for
From Flexible, their friend.

Flexible loves both Liberty and Law,
But being led by the Spirit
Is the most important thing of all.
He's at peace with himself,
But prays each night for Liberty and Law,
(For each have many talents),
That one day soon they'll learn to live
Together, peaceably in Balance.

The balance between liberty and law has been a struggle for God's people. Because there are so many situations that have no laws, we make choices for our own lives. That may be all right for us, but when we expect others to follow *our* rules, that is not all right.

A Deep Valley

There was a storm within my soul,
It cut me deep and made a hole.
It tormented me and left me sad,
It destroyed what little faith I had.

I stand alone and I feel
Darkness as it spins and reels,
'Round and 'round to make a web,
Leaving hope and victory dead.

Oh God, if You are really near,
Oh God, if You can really hear,
Let me see Your mighty hand
Reaching down to where I stand.
And let me know that You do care
For one lost soul who's in despair.

Pain and sorrow, troubles that come to each of us. Life happens. But the pain of life's trials can be more severe, more crippling, and more incapacitating than any physical pain because we look whole on the outside and are expected to carry on.

LOST DAY

You know the type of day I mean
When everything goes wrong.
You opened up your sleepy eyes
And there was a little song.

So gentle and so muted,
Against the roar of the day,
If, as a seed, I'd planted it,
I know it would have stayed.

But as the day moved onward
I didn't give a thought
To any power stronger than mine
And you know, I stayed on top.
That is, at least till ten o'clock,
And then my power stopped.

Why is it Lord, I don't hold fast
Each moment of my day?
I sometimes slip and forget it's You
That keeps me on the way.

And since Your grace was strong enough
To take Jesus to the cross,
It's strong enough to help me Lord,
On the days I feel are lost.

The beginning of each day is a new start, a new beginning, a time to start fresh. I think God knew that twenty-four hours was all we could handle without a fresh start. As we commit the beginning of each day to Him, He is faithful to give us what we need .

THE FOOLISH WOMAN

She loved her house,
It was her pride.
It was safe,
A place to hide
From winds and storms and wars of life,
Inside its walls there was no strife.

One day she noticed a window frame:
It didn't look right,
It wasn't the same
As all the other window sashes.
Trying to fix it
She created gashes
All along the painted wall.
And then she noticed that wasn't all.

She started working.
Each thing she tried
Disaster was lurking,
'Til in the end
Her house was a mess
Her heart was broken,
She had to confess.

The house she loved
No longer existed.
If only a carpenter's help were enlisted.
A carpenter trained and skilled in compassion
To fix things up in a suitable fashion.
Only when it needed to be done.
And as carpenters go, there's really just one
Who can fix things up and make them shine
And, of course, we know He's also divine.

A wise woman builds her house, while a foolish woman tears hers down by her own efforts.[Proverbs 14:1] We foolishly, by our own efforts, try to fix our house (spouse, children, self, etc.). Only God can create, but we become little gods and try to create the person we think is good. What heartaches. What disaster.

THE DUST SPEAKS

How arrogant I stand about
Thinking thoughts without a doubt.
There is no God and I can tell
I know it all so very well.
What I have I did myself.
There was no sitting on the shelf,
Waiting and praying on bended knee.
I tell you now that's not for me.
I'll take my chances when I die
There's no eternal by and by.

Oh, foolish man,
You are but dust.
For when you die,
And die you must.
Then too late your eyes will see
There is no life apart from Me.

How often we meet people who scorn faith. Puny man standing and defying the creator of galaxies; what a pitiful sight.

AS I BOW

As I bow before you, Lord
My eyes begin to see.
The world takes on a different light
When my heart's on bended knee.

As I bow before you, Lord
All defenses melt away.
It's me, just the way You made me,
With nothing much to say.

As I bow before you, Lord,
Eyes upon the ground;
And though the view is limited,
Insights there abound.

Humility before God, how it changes us. How it changes our outlook on life. Situations may not always change to our liking when we pray, but we always change when we bow our hearts before our Creator.

FOOLISH ME

God had a plan
I did not see;
Oh foolish, foolish me.
This plan demanded too much time,
It imposed on me and what was mine.
I decided to take another way.
God let me go, He didn't say,
"I won't permit it, you cannot go."
I didn't hear Him whisper "No."
But years went by,
Now too late I see;
Oh foolish, foolish, foolish me.

How often have we taken a detour from what God wanted for us? We have our plans. We are so sure of what we want. God lets us go. We learn. But I wonder, was there an easier way?

WISE MEN

Wise men laugh
And say You're not
Alive and watching from Your spot
On high, almighty ever-wise.
They say the Bible is just lies
Which are a crutch for people who
Cannot make a dream come true.

But God, I know it's You alone
Who made us all, sits on Your throne.
You made the wise who laugh at You.
But God, I'd like to say this to
All these wise but foolish men,
Who'll laugh their way unto their end.
If they are wise, then I can say,
I'm glad I'm dumb and know God today.

The Bible says "knowledge puffs up." Faith can't be explained, so some discredit it. "Thinking themselves wise, they become foolish." (Romans 1:22)

God's Presence

As my day takes shape
Softly from the early dawn,
Let me be aware of you, O God.
Let my first thoughts be of You,
My first words be spoken to my Creator.
In the foundation of my day,
May God be the solid rock I use.

In the hustle of my day
Scurrying toward its end,
Let me be ever sensitive to Your presence;
Allowing no harsh word or unkind action
To push You away.
In the midst of my hurried day
May Your presence be the transport I use.

At the end of my day
May your presence be as fresh
As it was at dawn.
That Your peace may have molded my day
Into something beautiful.
Another muted shade,
In the tapestry of my life.

Peace comes with His presence. In any situation, He can be there, but He comes by our invitation. How much more each day can be if we remember Him.

THE WALL

See this strong wall?
I built it so tall.
Each stone upon stone did I lay.
Every brick had a name
It's a why or a how
Or a fear or a vanity small.

Each one I laid down,
wouldn't hurt any ground.
But together made this fine wall.
Each one I laid down
Wasn't noticed or found
For I hid each new problem well,
'till a wall had been made
And the price I had paid
For no light gets to me now at all.

For each stone was set well
With doubt and mistrust,
And now I stand here alone.
For the love that He gave
I severed and made
A dungeon in which I dwell.

God never leaves us, but we often leave Him. Even if in attitude and only for an hour, it is much too long and much too far away.

A Tangled Situation

Father, it's so hard to think straight;
To see things from every angle.
So often the view we see
Depends on where we stand,
And a compromise isn't always possible.

I can't see things as You do,
For I don't know all things.
No matter how hard I try,
In some things I'm biased.
Help me to surrender my will to You.
Help me to become soft and not grow hard.
Help my attitude toward life be sweet.

May I lay my ashes before You, so that You
May in return give me beauty,
The beauty of Jesus.

Isaiah 61:3 "…to give unto them beauty for ashes"

Life is tough. How often we hear this. We have to make decisions that do not please everyone. Sometimes not even ourselves. Other people make choices that turn our world upside-down. Having the right attitude can save us much grief.

Believing You Love Me

Believing you love me
When I trip and fall;
Believing, to you,
It won't matter at all.

Believing you love me
When all looks black;
Believing and knowing
You won't turn your back.

Believing you love me
When I look like a fool.
Believing you love me
Because you're God's tool.

Believing you love me
And you'll understand.
Knowing it now
As you take my hand.

We need to feel accepted by others, especially fellow believers. However, the biggest stumbling-block to this is our own attitude.

THE VICTORY SONG

I love to change,
I love to change;
Completely made new
And all re-arranged.

When God touches something
He wants to make new,
I gasp and I think
Oh, what will I do?
Then He puts the desire
Down deep in my heart
Then speaks to me softly
"Now here's how to start."

As I step out
In this brand new way,
The joy that it brings
Causes me to say;
I love to change,
I love to change,
Completely made new
From bottom to top.

Oh! God in my heart
I say never stop
Cause me to change, Lord
Cause me to change.

The Spirit of God gives us the desire to change; to be something better than we were before we came to know Him. He also gives us the power and grace to change.

JESUS

From the tribe of Judah
Scripturally was proclaimed;
From the stem of Jesse,
Jesus Christ, He came.
Spoken Word of heaven,
Royal birth was He,
Image of the Father,
Here for us to see.

Worked with wood and hammer;
Building was His trade.
Knew He was superior,
Yet He humbly stayed,
Working and obeying
'till the time was here,
When His life He'd offer
For the ones so dear.

Cruelly, how they mocked Him—
It was you and me,
Showing how we hated
All His purity,
Took His broken body
Nailed it to a tree.
Broken with a world of sin
On Mount Calvary.

Capture all the beauty
Of a fine red rose;
Purity, His virtue
Yet our death He chose.
Yes, He died for you and me
Perfect offering,
Conscience-clear salvation
Through Jesus Christ our King.

On Being Smug

Did you ever have a day
That sometimes comes my way
When the pressures seem to squeeze
Upon your head?

When the things you thought were good,
Turned out not the way they should,
And left you feeling you didn't know
A thing?
Well, we look for reasons for this
And, I believe, that God implores us
To then, take a look or two inside our lives.

For we seem to get quite fixed,
And God then gives us a little mix
To make sure we don't settle in our ways.
For the moment we think we've arrived
At some eternal prize,
We have a tendency to settle back and smile.

But the things that we possess
Are worth something only if we confess;
I can live the way I do because
Christ strengthens me.

For the moment I think I have it
In my own strength, God will grab it
And I'm back to where I started—
Miry clay.

We have this treasure in earthen vessels. Without Him, we are simply earthen vessels. But with Him, we have a light and strength within. The light does not belong to the earthen vessel; we belong to the Light (2 Cor. 4:7).

FIRST LOVE

I feel I'm here at point A
Knowing His love just yesterday.
His grace is so real
His peace is so high
And really I can't understand why.

You see, I've been told
That I should be willing
To live in a mud hut
And make it my dwelling.
To go to the farthest parts of the earth
And lead many people to a spiritual birth.

Oh! When I heard this I got such a fright
Then to my possessions I clung very tight.
My spirit grew heavier with each passing hour,
My moods became oh so sour.
Then when the burden was heaviest of all
It was on Jesus's name I did call.

I told Him, "Lord, I feel like a mule;
I don't think I'm ready to be used as
God's tool.

But Lord, I give this burden to You
For I know there's nothing I can do
To change my heart and make it right."
To my surprise, I slept that night.

As I said, I'm at point A
Just knowing He loves me anyway.
His presence is real. I don't feel He's mad.
Oh, it makes my heart so glad.
But a funny thing is happening too,
Though I'm almost afraid to say it to you.

My thinking is changing,
I'm being transformed
As I look to Him whose body was torn.
It's strange, but the mud hut
Looks better each day
If only at His side I can stay.

God requires a quality of love from us that can only be described as "first love." With our eyes and hearts focused on Him, He can lead us easily in the way that is best for us.

FATHER

Father, that I can call You Father.
Creator of the galaxies is my Father,
Oh, can it be?
Father comes so easily to my lips
So much a part of my heart,
By Your Spirit You have made it so.
To call You Father would be foreign
To my mind
If Your Spirit wasn't born in me.
Now, calling You Father is instinctive
To my soul,
For You are indeed my Father.
And to think that You love me,
That I am precious in Your sight.
If I fully understood what that meant
Nothing could hurt me again.
I see in shadows now,
But, one day, I will know the extent
Of Your love.
For now, it is enough to call You Father.

How privileged we are that God wants to have a relationship with us. His love allows us to call Him Father.

ON BEING SPIRITUAL

Often in the Bible
We are reminded that
Praying in the closet
Is really where it's at.
Fasting should be secret
That folks will never know,
The good it will accomplish
May really never show.
Jesus told some people
Go from here, don't tell.
The healing was for just that one
They weren't to toll a bell.
Then, of course, our right hand
Should never look to see
If old lefty there is being
Just what he should be.
I think there is a message,
And it's done me good to know
That when I'm being "spiritual"
It should never really show.

Spirituality should not be worn as a badge of accomplishment.
Spirituality should be a natural outpouring of who we are when
God is in control of our lives.

MIXING THE WORD WITH FAITH

There once was a man,
A brilliant man,
I knew him very well.
He memorized the scriptures,
In quoting, he excelled.

In every situation
He had the verse to match.
In knowing verse and chapter
He wasn't one you'd catch.

He took a lot of pride in this
And wherever he would go,
He inspired people—
They often told him so.

But when he was in trouble
And feeling rather down,
No inspiration came to him
It just could not be found.

He knew he needed help
That was very plain,
But all he did about it
Was just wallow in his pain.

All the scriptures that he knew
Just rattled in his head.
If only he could get them
Into his heart instead.

Without faith, no man can please God. The Bible, though a wonderful book, will not change us unless the words are mixed with faith and dwell in our hearts.

HE IS THERE

Draw me near, oh God.
For only when I'm close to You
Do I see life in the right perspective.
The light you shine in my heart
Allows me to see;
The foolishness in the world's wisdom,
The wisdom in spiritual simplicity,
And a purpose in difficulties.
Your light reveals new concepts,
Your presence brings peace.
Close to God is where
The light is the brightest,
The wind the calmest,
And there is room for all.

How often we struggle and run looking for the peace that is so available. Take a moment, be quiet, and see He is there.

A NEW ME

I hunger and thirst for the Lord.
That's not a new feeling.
People throughout the ages have felt like that,
But, to me, it's new.
It's new to feel my soul extend upward
in search of God,
To see His hand in everything,
To sense His presence in every situation.
My soul is at peace.
My heart sings.
Surely this is the abundant life
Jesus spoke of.

Spiritual awareness has no age limit. This hunger can be in one very young or very old. It adds a dimension to our life that is personal, strengthening, and joyous.

Majesty and Simplicity (God and I)

Majestic and all-powerful,
Alone and complete,
Needing nothing;
God, my Father.

Creator of time,
Standing at its entrance.
He commanded the elements,
And created
Me, His child.

How can I relate
To my majestic and awesome Father?
He had even thought of that
And became a man, a Saviour,
Thank You, Father.

I see this awesome God and truly wonder how He could find me in this huge universe. I feel so small. Yet God finds us and is always with us and lifts us up to where He is.

THE TRAVELERS

Each person that came
Desired to please God.
Each person that came
Held in their hands a box.
Each box was a little different—
Some big and awkward,
Some were so small;
They could be held in one hand.
Others carried their box on their shoulders
And were weighed down by it.

None of the travelers looked happy
For this box was a great concern.
It must be defended against those
Who would think
That the box should be a different shape;
More like the one they themselves carried.
On they traveled,
Some looking smug,
Some looking unsure,
Others looking suspiciously about.
They came to a hill and stopped.
Boxes were gripped tightly,
Silence and tension filled the air.

Then, in the sky, a light appeared—
The definite shape of a cross.
Warmth radiated from the cross,
The travelers lifted their heads.
Boxes were dropped and forgotten
As hands were lifted in praise to their God.
Faces became radiant as they joined
Lifted hands to worship.
Love of God united the travelers.
They had come,
And God was pleased.

Religion can separate and divide, putting us in our individual boxes. How freeing it is to accept and love others as people of God, focusing less on the differences and more on the similarities.

COMPLETE SURRENDER

I cannot trust God unless
He is all-powerful.
I cannot believe in God unless
All truth is in Him.
I cannot completely relax
In my Saviour's arms unless
I know every situation is in His control;
That even the seemingly bad things
Are indeed from Him.
If I am in control of my destiny,
If my eternal salvation depends
In any way on me, or my strength,
Then God is less than
I need Him to be.

God can be trusted with our lives. Faith, of course, is the answer. Complete trust is the answer. Complete trust is essential. There is no question about God's ability.

HEAVY BURDENS

Slowly, slowly,
Letting go.
Releasing to God's hands
Precious burdens
That only He can carry.
Prayer and petitions
Lifted before His throne,
Laid down at His feet.
Then resting;
My head on His shoulder,
My confidence in His strength.

How tight we hold to our worries. As if worry alone could solve the problem. Even faith does not solve all problems. However, it does solve the problem of worry. It allows us to cope with problems that have no solutions.

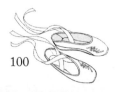

UNCONDITIONAL LOVE

What awesome love is this
That covers my sin in every
Area of my life?

What awesome love is this
That is never
Surprised by what I am?

What awesome love is this
That gives the greatest gifts
When I least deserve them?

What awesome love is this
That transforms me
Into what I cannot be on my own?

The story of the woman caught in adultery shows God's love in a way that surprises me by its limitlessness. We would think that a woman caught in adultery would be a situation God would surely condemn. But as I read this (John 8: 1-11), I see that the woman did not even repent before she was forgiven. She probably thought it would be useless. God's love is so all-encompassing, it is truly awesome.

Easter Poem

Satan laughed.
Christ was dead.
The Saviour of mankind,
Lifeless on a tree.
Now there would be no Saviour.
Humanity was doomed with Satan
And he rejoiced.

Mankind cried.
Jesus had been their hope;
A king to worship,
A friend,
A redeemer,
But He was dead.
Crucified, flesh and blood,
Without power, without hope.

Then they saw Him
Risen just as He'd said.
He was alive.
Victor over death;
Faith returned,
Hope everlasting.
He was who He claimed to be;
The risen Saviour.

Rejoice, celebrate,
And with thanksgiving
Realize that I am also risen.
His power dwells in me.
I am risen to new life.
Power over sin;
The risen Christ in me.

As we celebrate our risen Lord, remember there was a time when there was no hope; no promise of eternity. Let us not take for granted this unfathomable gift.

GOD SAW YOU THERE

God saw you there;
Doing good, being good, trying hard.
It was a struggle,
But you did it,
Every hour, ever day, every year.

God saw you there;
He loved you too much
To leave you there.
He had so much more for you,
But you didn't need Him.
You were doing good.

God saw you there
When it happened.
It all fell apart.
You couldn't do it any longer.
Not without help,
Not without God.

God saw you there.
He was waiting,
Without judgment, without condemnation,

Only loving and longing
To lead His child to a better way;
A way of grace,
An abundant life full of joy,
God leads you there.

We try so hard. We were never meant to do it without God's help. God has to break us before we are free to know His grace. Then we find His rest.

Regrets

Opportunities have gone,
Chances to do good,
Chances to point in God's way.
My way was better.
Or was it?
If another path was taken,
What would I have been?
What would my children have been?
But it's gone,
Gone, never to be redone.

But God was watching,
Ever loving,
Ever holding out His hand.
Directing your path,
As He directs your children's path now.

Beauty for ashes.
Righteousness is not earned,
Salvation cannot be bought with good behaviour.
God freely gives to all who ask,
Whenever they ask.
Good and bad stand equal in God,
Receiving a gift

From a Father who gives to all,
No respecter of persons,
Not preferring one above the other.

Wishing we had done things differently is a waste of energy. God can turn every decision we have made for our good when we look to Him by faith.

The Greatness of God

How great You are,
That You can see
Beauty in this soul called me.

How merciful You must be,
That You can forget
What I used to be.

How wise You are
That You can see
Usefulness in this soul called me.

As I stand before my Creator, the realization of all He is fills me,
and I feel so small. Yet He loves me and sees me as someone valuable.

ALONE

Life has given me much
And I am grateful.
Riches are to be enjoyed,
Bringing much satisfaction.
But the essences of life
Does not spring from riches.
Peace and satisfaction
Come from an inner stability
That only God can give.
Knowing that
As all things fall apart,
He holds me in His hand
And has promised,
Never to leave me alone.

This was written for everyone that did not have a good view.
(See poem "The View")

Beauty for Ashes

Injustice prevails,
Violence rules,
The innocent suffer,
And God waits.

Prayers are offered,
Sacrifices made,
Pleading hearts seek,
And God waits.

Waits with an everlasting patience,
Waits with infinite wisdom,
That sees the end
When His justice will prevail.
"Vengeance is mine," saith the Lord,
"I will repay."

And He does repay;
Beauty for ashes,
Mercy for violence,
Life for death.

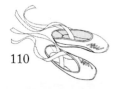

God is so tolerant of His creation. He waits and waits and the helpless suffer. I don't understand. Yet He is a God of love who has made an eternal way for anyone who seeks it.

PRAY ON

From a dark, lonely prison cell,
Words of prayer are offered.
Forces shift in the spiritual realm,
No one notices,
Pray on.

From a sick bed
Where the world is kept at bay by pain.
Prayer arose for those around,
Peace enters, stress reduced, hearts are softened.
The change is taken for granted,
No one notices,
Pray on.

From a million corners
Arise a silent army of words.
On a heavenly throne, a Father listens,
Aware of every word.
The world is changed,
In small ways,
In great ways,
And no one notices.
Pray on.

A connection may never be made by others when we pray in any situation. We ourselves can give praise to the One who answers. I believe God does not always want us to be ringing the bell to give Him credit. He will work quietly in His own way. He is a humble God. He is able to reach people.

Conversation with God

"God, sometimes I'm selfish,
And only think of me."
"I know, and I still love you."

'I think mean thoughts
About good people."
"I know, and I still love you."

"The ones I love most,
I hurt, and I don't say I am sorry."
"I know and I still love you."

"There are times I'm afraid
And I lash out because I don't know
Who my friends are."
"I know and I still love you."

"At weak moments,
I don't do the right thing."
"I know, and I still love you."

"Sometimes I have murderous thoughts
Toward God and man.
I feel no one could ever love
Someone like me,
But You know, and You still
Love me, right?"
"Yes"
"Teach me to love that way."

God is love. He never changes. We can't imagine this. We feel God must be angry with us or tired of us. By His grace we can be more like Him—kinder, more patient, non-judgmental, forgiving.

Singing His Song

God's love grows strong within me,
Through trouble great and small.
How it actually comes about,
I do not know at all.
When I look within myself,
A love that's not from me
Is showing love to others
And I think, how can it be?
They're not the kind of person
To whom I would be drawn,
But as I think a little more,
The light begins to dawn.
The Spirit of God within me
Wants the world to see His love.
My arms are now the arms of God
With a purpose from above.
So listening to His urging,
I follow right along,
Learning the words as I go;
To the world I sing His song.

When we feel compassion, I believe it is from God. When we have a relationship with God, He wants to move through us. All we have to do is respond. The freer we are from negative emotions, the easier it becomes to sing the words of His song to the world.

WINGS

I prayed, "God, ease her suffering,"
It seemed to intensify.
I prayed, "God, take her early,"
When He didn't, I wondered why.

God is being cruel, I thought.
I didn't understand.
But the Creator of the universe
Had another plan.

The suffering seemed so senseless,
Completely without cause.
Then God showed me a picture
That made me stop and pause.

A butterfly was struggling,
Leaving its cocoon.
It struggled and it suffered,
There just wasn't enough room.

The wings it carried on its back
Were big and cumbersome.
It'd surely die from this great test.
I wanted to help, so it could rest.

But God, in His great wisdom
Knew the fight would make it strong.
To cut the suffering short,
Really would be wrong.

It'd be stronger from the struggle,
One day fly high and free.
I really would have hurt it,
If it were left to me.

So my friend keeps struggling on,
Her heavenly wings grow large and strong,
Until one day with God she'll sit,
Her glorious wings will then just fit.

"...to make the captain of their salvation perfect through sufferings" (Hebrews 2:10). Even though I believe we must ease any suffering, I believe it has to be part of God's eternal plan. Hard times make us strong if we look to God. Sickness is a different kind of suffering, but I believe if we see a purpose in it, we can endure it better and have hope.

Subtle Sin

A good man had a garden,
An evil man had one beside.
The good man loved his garden,
The evil man despised
The efforts of the good man,
So a plan he did devise.

He mixed a little poison
In the water one fine day
And soon he hoped that he would see
The good man's land decay.
The evil man used poison
That was slow acting, yes indeed,
For it didn't really kill the plants
It just twisted up their leaves.

People came from miles around
To see the twisted leaves.
They thought it quite unusual
"How original," they said.
But even though it looked alive,
The good man knew, it's dead.

Years went by and this kind of death
Spread from leaf to leaf
Till every flower on the earth,
Had these twisted leaves.

People thought it normal
No one would complain,
But the good man sold his garden
For he couldn't stand the pain.

A lesson can be learned from this
And I hope we come to know,
A little bit of poison
Will twist us as we grow.
The beauty that we could attain
Will never ever show.

121

No one will know the difference
We may fool everyone,
Only the Gardener looking down
Will know the damage done.

We are all like Adam and Eve thinking one bite won't hurt us. But good is the enemy of the best. Dabbling in the things we already know will hurt us can change us in ways we are not aware of.

Tough Love

Fear was my mentor
Showing me how to live,
Teaching me to step carefully.
Calamities were avoided
With fear as my mentor.

Then fear let me down.
Choices made by others
Sent my life out of control.
My troubles multiplied
With fear as my mentor.

I ran but fear caught me,
I struggled but fear bound me.
There was no comfort or peace
With fear as my mentor.

Broken and beaten
My strength was all gone.
I was hopeless and alone
With fear as my mentor.

At last the face of fear
I finally saw.
I turned and chose love.
Fear faded into shadows
With love as my mentor.

My chains fell off
My heart was free.
God had allowed
The worst of life
To destroy my mentor, fear.

Tough love doesn't always feel like love. God allows trouble in our lives but I feel it is from a heart of love. He longs for us to be free from the things that bend and twist our lives.

THE POWER OF PRAYER

Death stepped forward and said,
"I will take these two,
Away from family and friends,
They will come with me now."
God saw and sent His people to pray.

In a instant their lives
Were claimed back from death.
But death was persistent
He waited and watched.
God's people waited and prayed.

Golden bowls in heaven
Were filled with prayers.
These were precious to God.
The prayers created a perfume,
Soft and light.
Filling the heavens
And surrounding the two,
Where they lie sleeping.

The golden bowls of prayer
Were filled and overflowed,
Creating channels by which
God could bless and heal.

Death took one step back,
Then two, three, and was gone.
In death's place, God's angels
Surrounded the two
Bringing peace and healing.

This poem was written about two young girls severely injured in a car accident which almost claimed their lives. Prayer and faith played a big part in their recovery.

IN SUPPORT OF MEN

Eve was out for a walk in the garden one day,
Alone, without Adam she decided to stray,
To the forbidden tree that intrigued her so,
Its beautiful fruit hung heavy and low.
She just wanted to look and maybe find out,
Why this fruit was forbidden
While God wasn't about.

The devil had seen Eve's inquisitive eyes,
If he wanted to trap her, he'd do it with lies.
So Satan to fool her took on a disguise.
In his snake form, to Eve he spoke soft and low.
"Did God say you'd die from this fruit? Oh no,no,no.
I've eaten it plenty and see how I shine,
My skin's slippery and sleek.
Come let us dine."

So Eve listened with interest,
Then took a big bite,
Gathered some fruit,
Then walked home for the night.
When Adam saw her
She did not look the same,
Her body was covered,

127

He thought, *It's a game.*
Then he looked in her eyes
And there he saw shame.

He knew in an instant,
This would change his life,
But the thought that came stronger was,
Eve is my wife.
The fruit that she carried
Was forbidden and wrong.
He thought for a moment
But it didn't take long.
The bite that he took tasted sour and strong.

The rest is history as they say,
No one knows what
Adam thought that day.
But God made Adam
Protective and strong,
Was he thinking of Eve
When he chose to do wrong?
What would have happened
If she'd sinned alone?
Flesh of his flesh,
Bone of his bone.

Did the vision of Eve
That flashed through his head,
Frighten and hurt him
And fill him with dread?
Did he love Eve
As Christ loves his bride?
Did he stand and hold her
And together they cried?
Did they walk from the garden
Together as one?
And as God watched them walk out
Did he think of His Son?

It is interesting to see Adam as a type of Christ sacrificing himself for his bride. Adam is sometimes portrayed as weak and henpecked for taking the bite of the apple. I think he deserves more credit. Eternity holds the answer.

WE THE PHARISEES

Give me freedom, freedom we cry,
Freedom is what we crave,
Freedom from the prisons of life,
Prisons that man has made.
Prisons of tradition,
Prisons of conform,
We become the Pharisees
That dictate the norm.
Jesus gave us freedom.
He said "I'm the light, the way."
Freedom from all prison cells,
Changing night to day.
But we surely don't believe Him,
He surely can't be right.
Throw out all tradition,
Put conformity to flight?
Is Jesus really all we need,
Him and Him alone?
Surely there is some method,
Some compromising form;
Read the Bible through each year,
Pray three times a day,
Go to church on Sunday,
Walk the narrow way.
Good things become tradition
If we leave out a vital part.

Good things become conformity
Without a seeking heart.
A heart that thirsts for Jesus,
Without Him feeling torn.
Such hearts tradition cannot convert.
Such hearts by the Spirit are born.
Born in freedom to serve Him .
Born without their Sunday best.
So, if we Pharisees will let Him,
I'm sure God can do the rest.

Judging others is so easy. We look on the outside. Only God can see the heart. We can all clean up good, but it can be a mask. Transformation takes place on the inside, slowly. Sometimes we can't see it. It's not our place to judge others or try to change them.

JESUS WAS A REBEL

What would Jesus do?
Can lead you astray,
'cause Jesus was a rebel
By the standards of today.

He didn't go to church each Sunday,
He didn't cut His hair,
He even worked on holy days—
Pharisees beware!

He spat in soil and healed with mud,
He said salvation was by His blood,
Eat His body, could this be right?
Many left the fold that night.

He forgave a woman, who didn't repent,
He said His words where heaven sent,
He spent time with lepers, sinners too,
This was something you should do.

But Jesus was a rebel
With one purpose on His mind.
Jesus was a rebel
The loving, caring kind.

His purpose was love
Which will always endure.
What would Christ do?
Can we really be sure?

Listening to the still small voice in our hearts takes a real relationship with a living God. This is what God wants, to be able to lead and guide us by His peace, not by dos and don'ts. Even though the law is good, relationship is better.

SIN TAKES PRISONERS

He was captured, hands and feet tied,
And dragged away to an area deep in the forest.
He was locked in a cage, like an animal,
Ropes tying him down,
Given a little food, water and left to die.

His friends didn't even know he was in trouble.
But now, they knew he needed help.
They didn't know where to look.
They didn't know how to help.

Then one day, there was news about him.
His friends had an idea.
They had the tools needed to release him.
The tools were a little rusty from lack of use;
Nevertheless, they took hatchets and knives,
Machetes and axes.

At first, the way into the forest was dense.
It looked like they were making little difference,
But they were persistent.
Slowly a path was cleared.
They were able to see the prison that held him,

The ropes that bound him.
He was alone and near death.

They used their tools to break down the prison,
To loose his bonds.
He was free, but helpless.
They carried him to safety, fed and washed him;
Slowly life returned to him.
His friends protected him with their strength
Until he was strong enough to protect himself.

Why did it happen?
What led him to captivity and bondage?
His friends never knew,
But they were persistent in their search,
Single-minded in their purpose,
And the simple tools they had were enough.

Such is prayer.
Simple,but enough.
Enough to break the bondage,
Enough to set the captives free.
His friends are us.
We may be the only thing
Standing between

Captivity and freedom,
Life and death.
Pray, and go forth.

Circumstances of life overtake people. Depression, addictions, and bad choices can lead us down a path that we can become stuck in. Praying friends can help in ways that nothing else can.

MURDOCK

Murdock was so loving,
As loving as could be.
Everywhere that Murdock went,
It was plain to see
That Murdock left some happiness
Joy and peace behind.
Murdock didn't have a lot
But Murdock sure was kind.

Murdock prayed for a gift from God,
Something he could do
To show the Lord he loved Him
And help a soul or two.
Although he waited patiently
Nothing seemed to come,
So sometimes to Murdock
Life seemed a little glum.

Time went by from day to day
With Murdock spreading cheer.
Others saw that he was gifted,
But Murdock sometimes feared
That God would not be pleased with him
For he didn't do enough.

Because of this, for Murdock
Life was sometimes rough.

Days and months turned into years,
Then Murdock's life was gone.
Murdock stood before the Lord
And asked Him what went wrong.
"I prayed for a gift to help You,
Something I could do
To show the world You love them
But now my life is through."

Jesus looked at Murdock
And said, *"Well done, my son.
I gave you the gift of helping,
And you've multiplied it some.
Every smile and kindness
You gave away so free,
Every sacrificial helping
Was a little bit of me."*

Kindness seems like a small thing, but kindness, if shown
consistently, can change relationships, save marriages, and make the
world a whole lot nicer place to live.

Miscellaneous

To My Children

If you achieve no great feats,
If you attain no great status,
Your life will be of immeasurable value
If each day you live in peace and kindness.
If each decision you make is from
A soft and humble heart,
If your purpose toward mankind is to do no harm,
If your pleasures are in simple things;
So easily found
So easily missed,
If your legacy is honesty,
If your children's inheritance is integrity,
Then no greater honour could you
Bestow upon me.

Not everyone can hold great positions in life. But everyone, in their own way, can be great.

ALL THAT YOU WILL BECOME

Emerging from the old, I see
You are becoming something new.
Discarding the worthless,
Salvaging the priceless,
Creating, with grace,
Someone that never was;
Someone of immense value.
With purpose, you explore new ground,
With caution, you test,
With humility, you accept
Attitudes and values
That become part of you.
With peace, you survey
All that you have gained,
All that you have discarded,
And you continue to move forward.
In love, I watch.
In gratefulness, I enjoy.
In confidence, I anticipate
All that you will become.

If we watch closely, we can see people struggle and change. This was written for my husband. With four children to raise, we have both had to change a great deal. I always appreciate the effort he puts into becoming a better husband and father, loner that he is.

THE STRENGTH OF FRIENDSHIP

The strength of friendship
Is not measured
By good times together,
Common interests,
Or even years of relationship.

Friendships, if not valued
Will be lost.
For friendships are made up of people,
None perfect,
None without flaws.
And in time may hurt or offend;

Then is the strength of friendship measured.
Then is the value of this person made known to us.
Do we turn our backs,
Or is this friendship
Important enough to suffer for;
A little or maybe a lot?

Is this friendship
Strong enough to withstand
The turbulence that circumstances can bring?

Strong enough to fold the sharp edges
of misunderstanding
Under the gentleness of love,
And still remain friends?

My friend of many years did something that so disappointed me, I drew back and didn't want to see her. She was in a town a couple of hours away, so it was easy not to see her. One day she called and asked me if there was a problem. I could not lie to her as we had been friends too long. I remember her saying, "You weren't even going to tell me? You were just going to close the door on me?" She was right. It was then I realized that true friends are worth fighting for.

WHY?

Damaged people,
Hurt by circumstances of life,
Crippled, maimed,
Testimonies of how cruel life can be.
To say that God is love,
And He allows this?

From the smallest hurt,
To the greatest atrocity,
He could have prevented it.
He is, *if* He is, all powerful.
If He is limited, then He isn't God.
But life itself testifies to His existence.

Therefore, why?
Is not metal heated by fire
So it can be bent?
Is not gold and silver put through fire
So the impurities will rise and be skimmed off?
Is not human character stronger
When it has been through the fire?

143

Life is that fire,
Heated by God's love,
To bring out the best in us.
With Him as our compass
We can navigate the torrents of life,
Avoiding some, but steering straight through others,
Gaining wisdom and strength,
Leading the way for others.

"Why" is such a big question. Sometimes nothing makes any sense. It takes faith to trust God. But really, is there a better alternative when things are beyond our control?

GUILTY

From the moment I saw your face
I was smitten.
Captured forever by a child
Who asked for nothing,
But to whom I would give the world
If I could.

I wanted you to be warm,
So I clothed you.
I wanted you to grow,
So I fed you.
I wanted you to do well,
So I held you and sang to you.

As you grew
I encouraged you to dress warmly,
I insisted that you eat well,
And yes, I nagged you instead of singing,
All from the same heart of love.

As I look at your adult face now,
I am still smitten.
I still want to give you the world.
And if this love has made you weak,
Unable to face or conquer your world,
Then yes, blame me,
I'm guilty.

Can we love our children too much? Does love make them weak? Discipline is a necessity, I know. Where is the balance? Difficulties can build character. They need to struggle to become strong. Where is the balance?

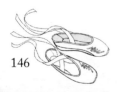

TRUTH

When truth is negotiable,
There is no foundation.
Whether in family or nation
Everything is up for grabs,
Bribes become a way of life,
Trade-offs a necessity.
Honour does not exist,
Trust, a word without meaning.
Truth and integrity
Must walk hand-in-hand.
Without them,
The world dissolves
Into an uncivilized state.
It may still have
All the glitz and glamour,
But the foundation is missing.
Nothing solid can be built.
Survival of the fittest prevails.
Animal instincts rule,
And no one is safe for long.

My husband and I support a missionary who has given his life to help the poorest of Africa. "Throw-away babies" is how he started. He has had to fight corruption in the highest levels to even stay alive.

THE ENEMY IN OUR MIDST

It lives among us
Eating, working, sleeping,
But it will never be
One of us.

Its heart is hidden
By a mask
That smiles and speaks,
Revealing nothing of the evil
In its heart.

Such coldness and hate
Remaining day after day,
Year after year,
Studying for destruction.
It closes its eyes to good.

The good that must overcome evil,
The good that must protect,
The good that must seek justice,
The good of all that must prevail,
The good that separates us from *It*.

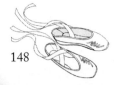

This was written after the attacks on the World Trade Center. But I can see that evil of any kind works the same way, sometimes disguising itself as good.

LOVE AND HATE

Hate has fiery eyes,
A face of fury,
And appears strong.

Love casts its eyes down,
Soothing the hurts of a child,
And appears weak.

Hate, with a strength
Found in madness,
Destroys and knocks down.

Love, with a strength
Found in meekness,
Restores and builds up.

Hate holds a grudge
That eats away at itself,
Becoming an empty shell.

Love seeks justice and forgiveness
That feeds its soul,
Growing stronger,
Until love
Can nourish the nations.

God uses the weak things of this world to confound the wise. We often do not understand His ways. When we are weak, then are we strong. Love does not appear to be strong on the outside, but what inner strength it requires to accomplish it.

A NURSE (A GIVER)

A warm smile—Acceptance
A cool cloth—Comfort
A moment spent—Concern
Relieving pain—Rest
Things that are all within
My grasp to give.

Every day, as a nurse
I have opportunities to affect lives
In a positive way;
People that I would never have met,
People opening their lives,
Allowing me in to give.
As a result, I receive
Many times, far more.
Lighting the corner where I live—
There is no greater privilege.

CONTROL

Life is not about who's right,
Getting what you want.
Life is about compromise,
Loving and giving.
About how to live with yourself,
Without anger or resentment.

Other people's decisions affect me.
When we make a compromise
That we can both live with,
There is peace.
I must let go of any control.
They must live with their consequences.
I must live with mine.

If there is no compromise,
No giving up of control,
On one or both sides,
I must walk away
With my choice.
I can't control them.
My attitude must be,
Peace be with you.
This is what I must do for me.

Our behaviour shows how wise we are. Do we sit and nurse old wounds like they are rare treasures? All that oozes from old wounds is poison. Let go, forgive, have peace. God's grace enables us to do this.

THE CREATION OF LAUGHTER

Before time began
Joy had no outlet,
No outward expression of itself.
Without this,
Joy really did not exist.

Emotion itself needed
A form of expression.
'Round and 'round
Up and down it went.
Nothing to guide it
Nothing to hold it steady.

Each was an entity unto itself,
Moving in its own orbit.
Circling, circling,
Without purpose,
Creating nothing.

A divine hand moved
Causing their orbits to collide.
A loud sound filled the universe,
Pleasant waves vibrated
From star to star.

155

The heavenly beings
Listened and approved.
It was pleasant.
It was uplifting.
Joy and emotion had met.

Laughter was born
The heavens were filled
With this new delightful sound.
Laughter, one of God's
Gifts to mankind.

Humor is such a vital part of life. If any relationship is to survive, it needs laughter. I love this picture of laughter being created. The whole universe laughing together. I would love to be a part of such joy.

LITTLE WORRIES

Little worries
Creep into my mind,
Weaving a pattern of dread,
Blocking out hope.

Little worries
Steal away joy,
Leaving heaviness,
Silencing laughter.

Little worries
Rob my life of energy,
Grieving fills my soul,
For things that never happen.

How silly we are to allow little worries to rob us of our joy. When we have no big worries we often find little ones to dwell on. Gratefulness is the cure. Gratefulness for all we now have.

THIS CHOICE

This choice that I did not make
Affects me as if
I had made it myself.
All the disappointment
Comes to me,
All the heaviness
Following a bad decision,
All the dreams evaporating
Into nightmares,
Sadness shadowing me
Like a faithful puppy.
This choice that I did not make.
This choice that was made
By someone I love.

Our lives can be sent into a tailspin by someone we love making a wrong choice, a bad decision. It's totally beyond our control but we suffer anyway.

THE TRUTH IN LOVE

Truth, you say, is important.
I too will agree
Truth is the most important thing,
It's a defense for you and me.
Shout it from the rooftops,
Let everybody hear;
We stand for truth and rightness
Then we need not ever fear.
But wait a little moment,
Before on our high horse we get,
There is a little more to this
I hope we won't forget.
The truth, in love, is more complete
For the truth is right,
But not always sweet.
So let your spirit rule your head,
Speak truth, in love, instead.

I often feel so passionate about something because I know it's right. But the person to whom I'm speaking is flesh and blood. Circumstances do not change what's right, but love covers a multitude of sins. Love is supreme. We need not ignore the truth, but let our words be wrapped in love, compassion, and understanding. Ephesians 4:15 "But speaking the truth in love…"